Balance

Angie's Extreme Stress Menders

Volume 1

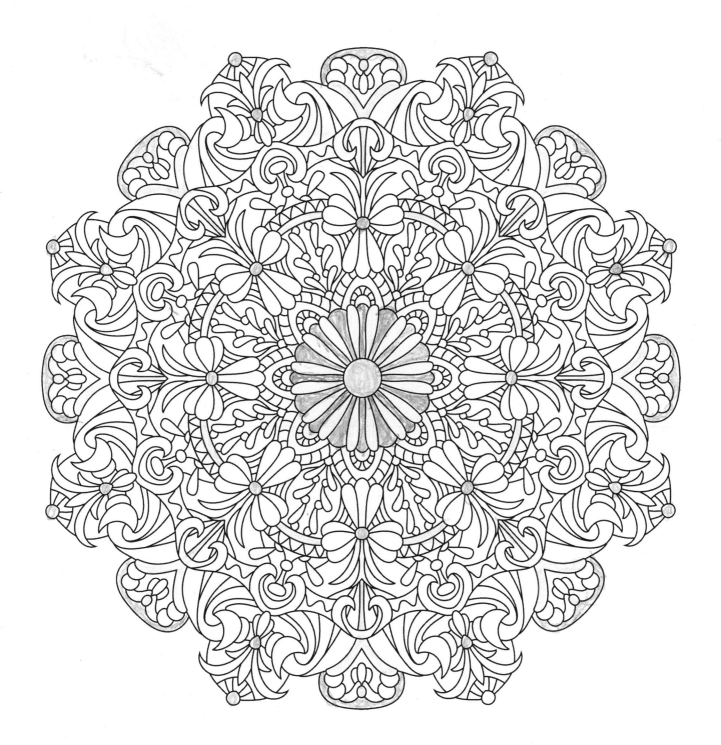

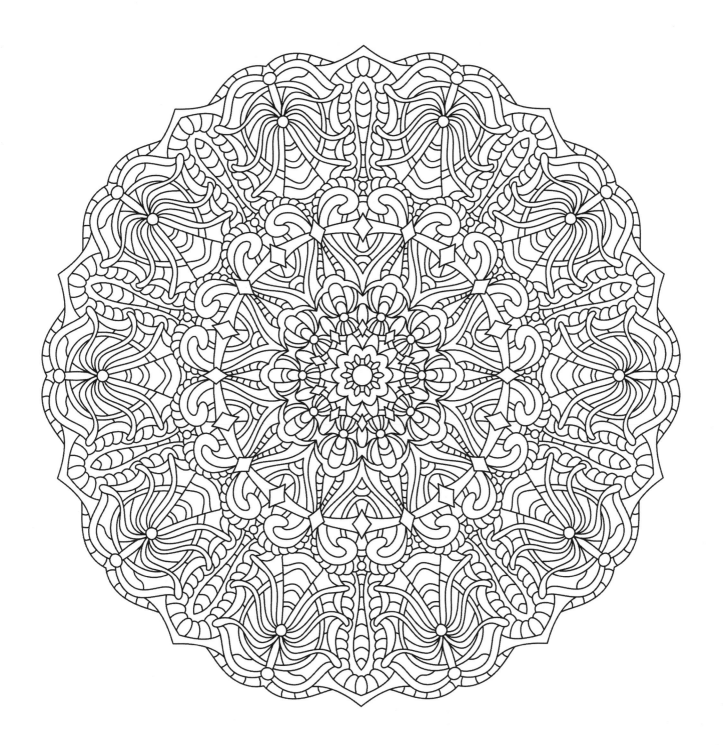

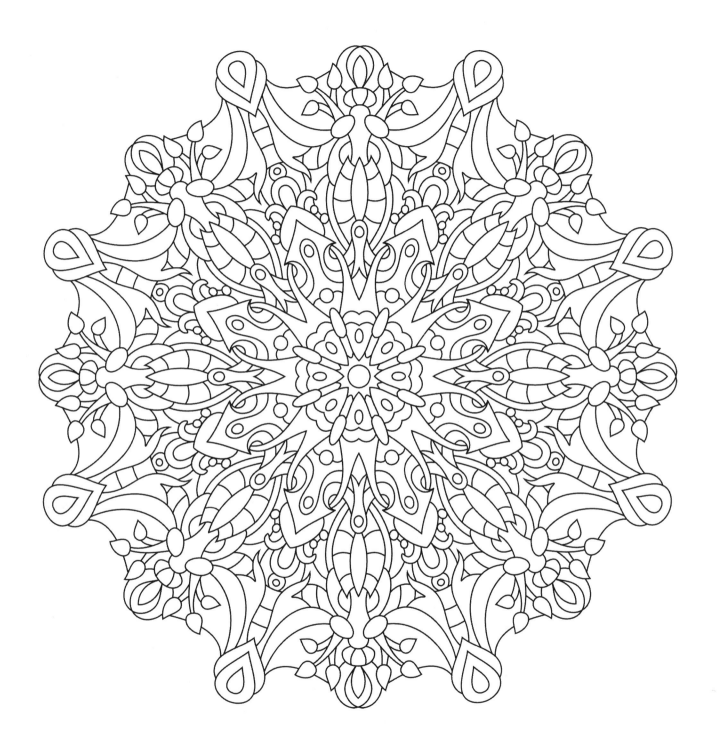

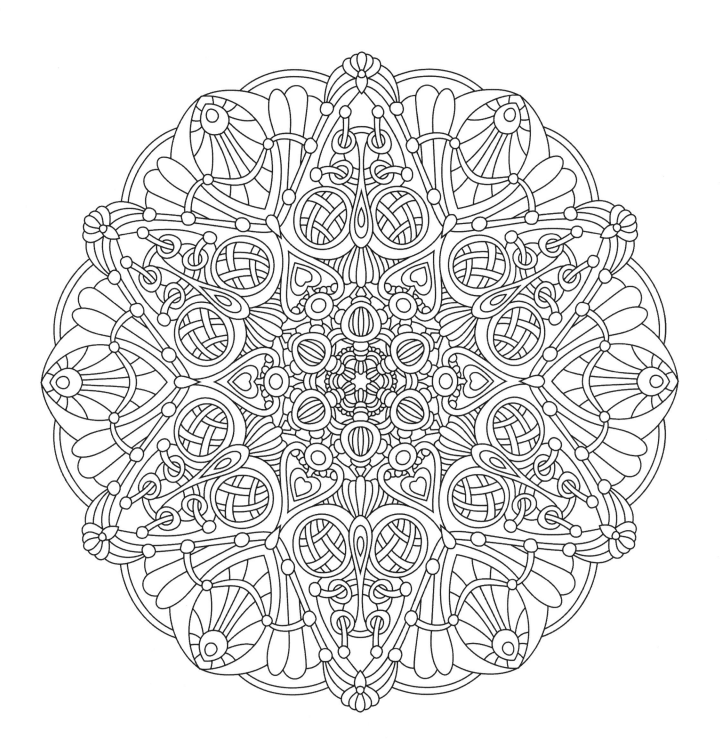

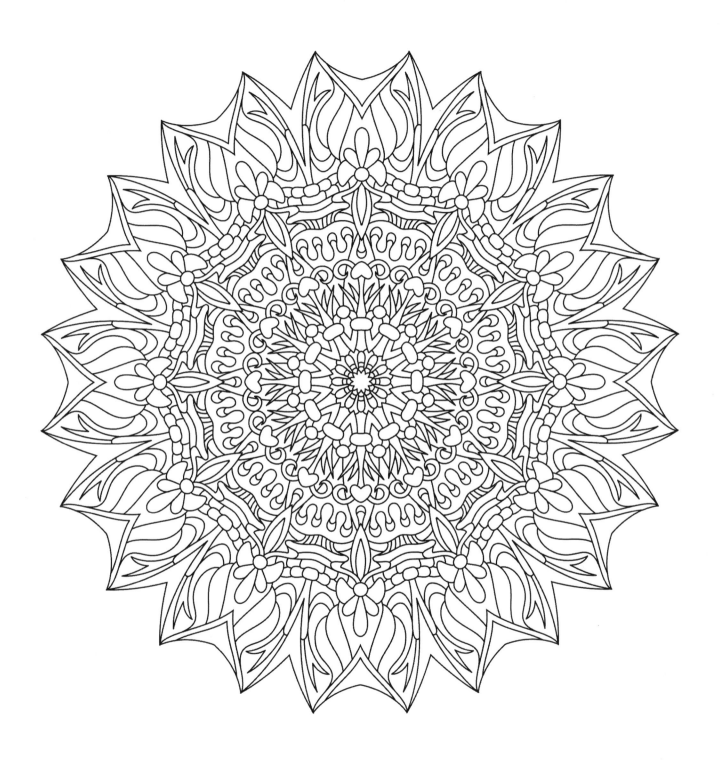

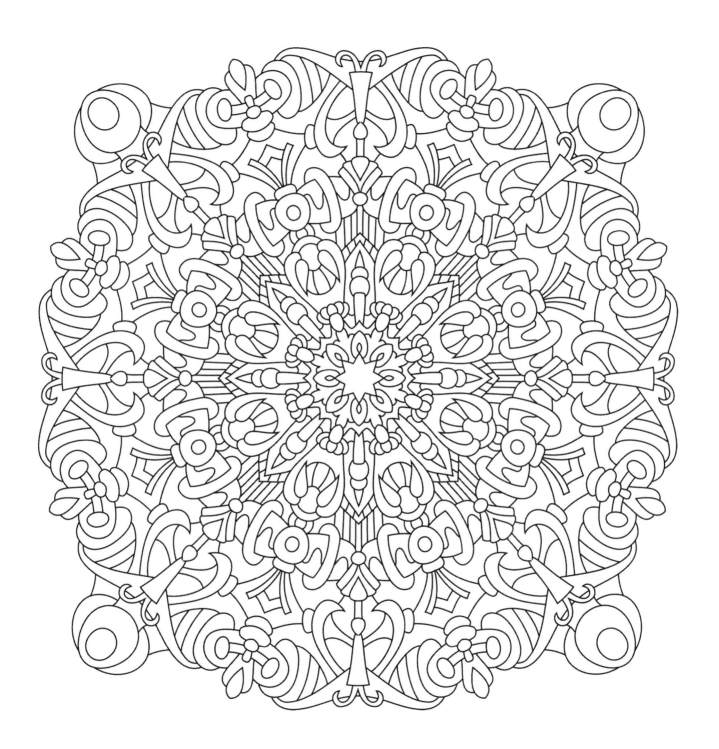

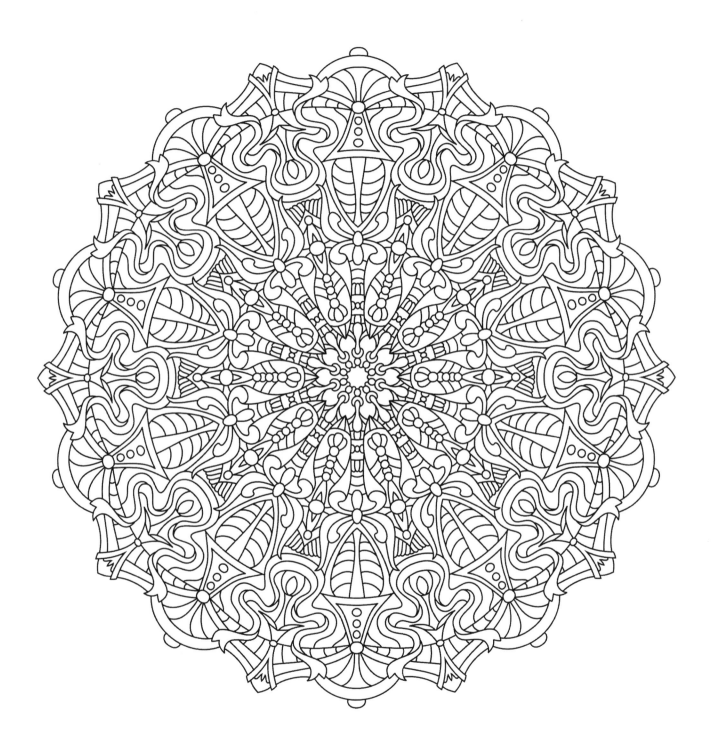

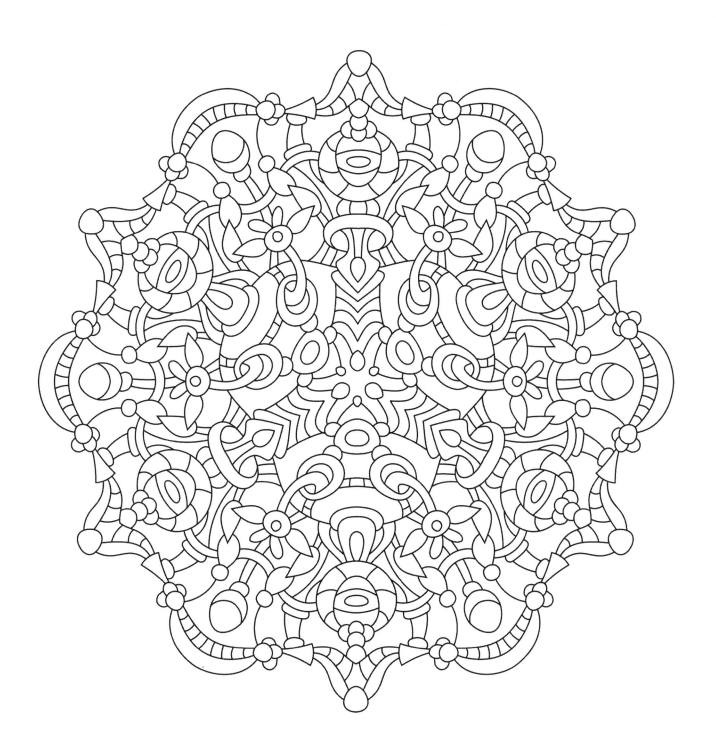

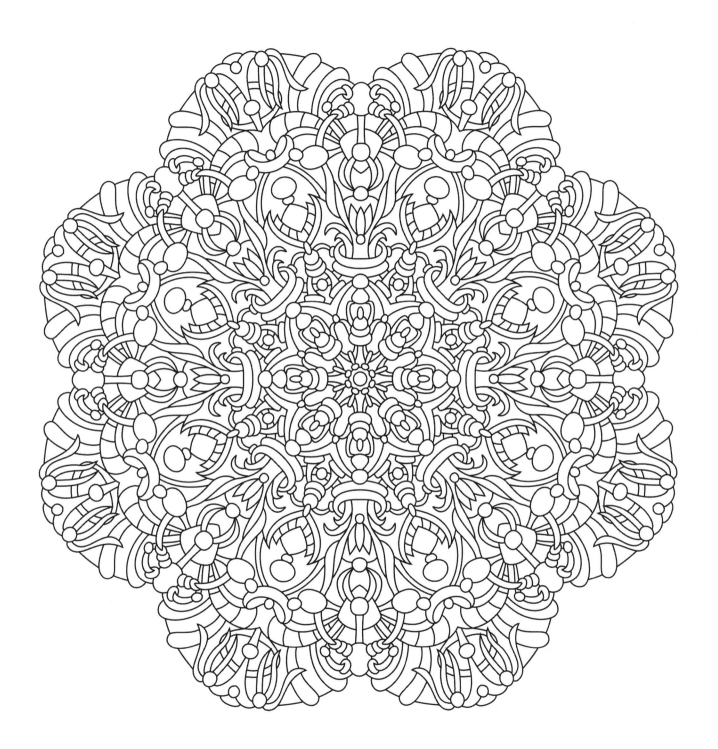

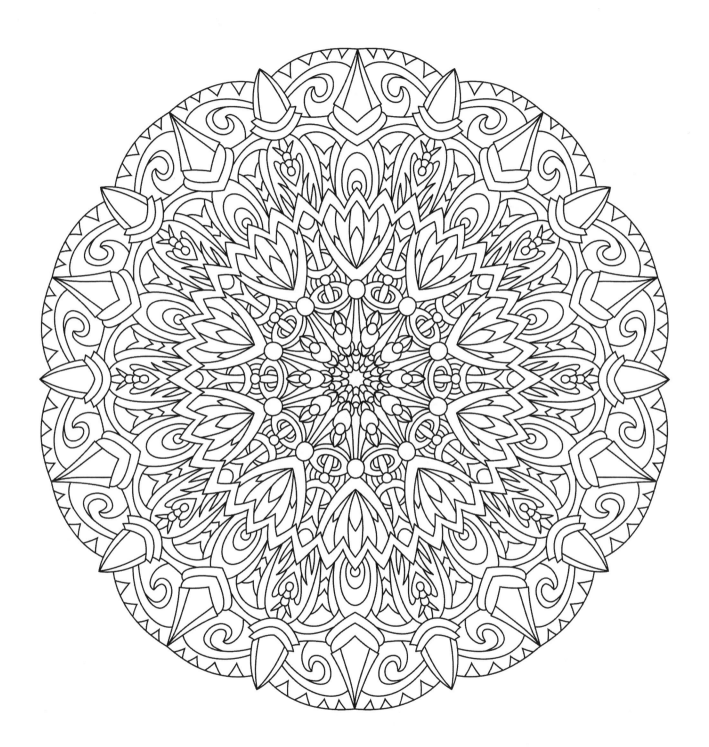

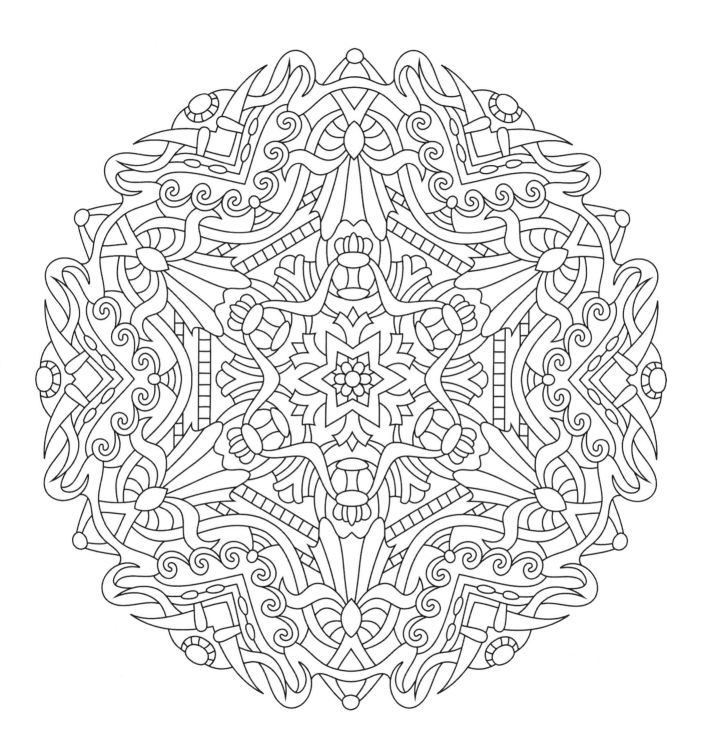

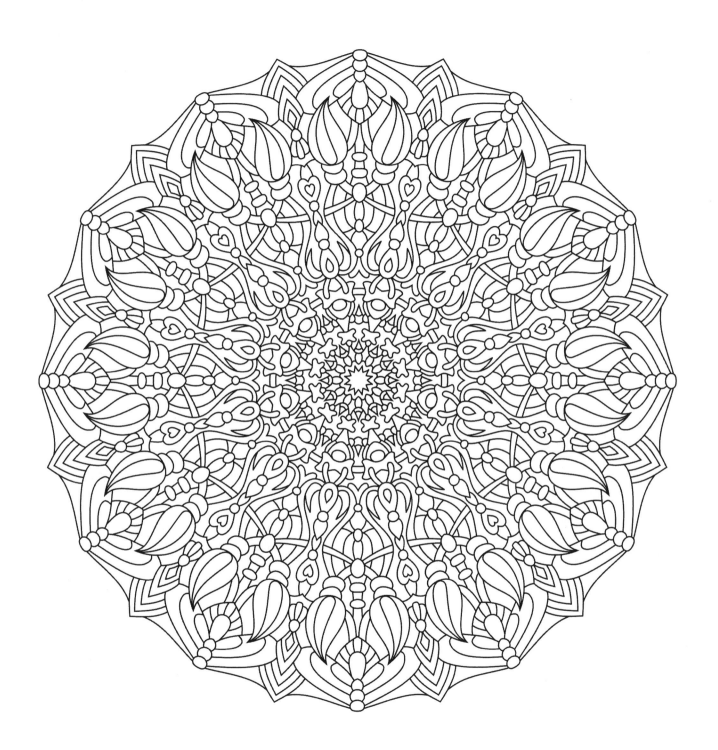

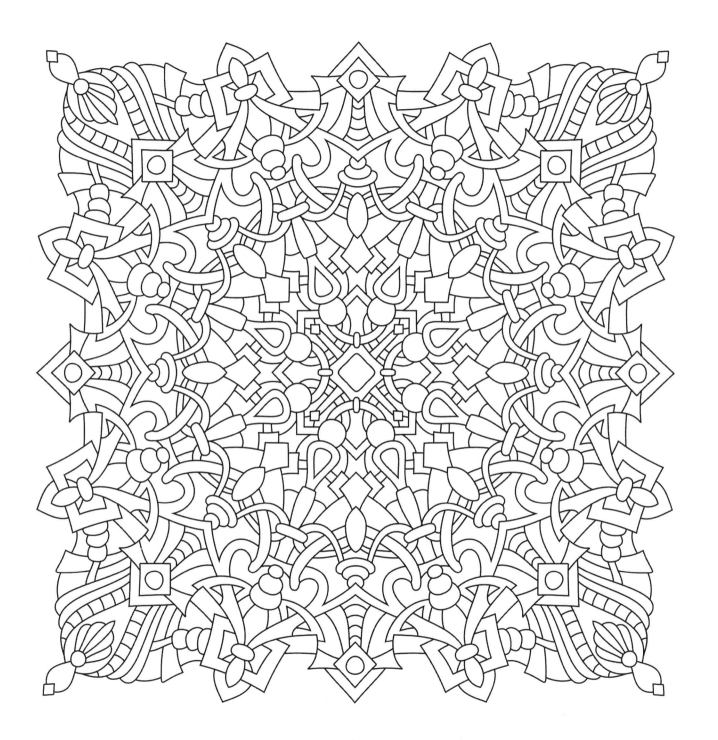

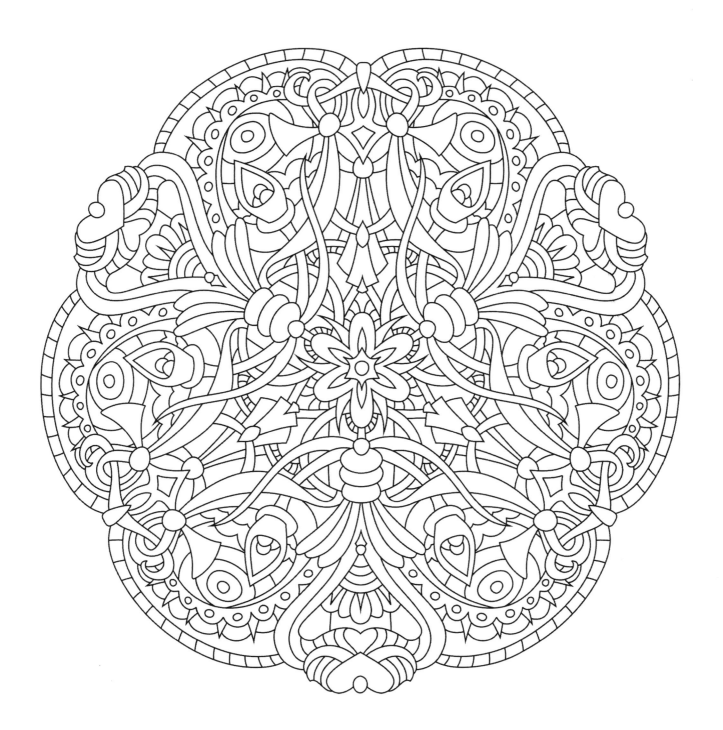

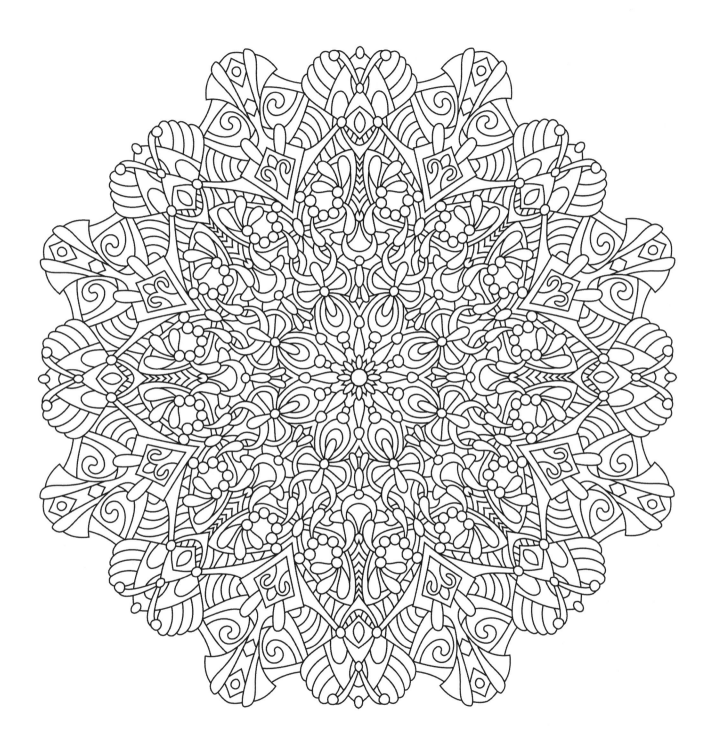

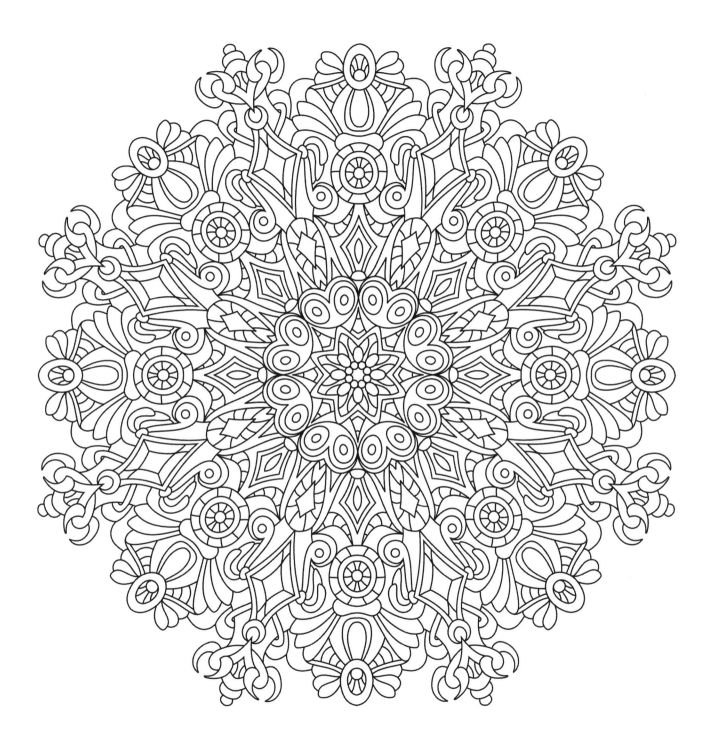

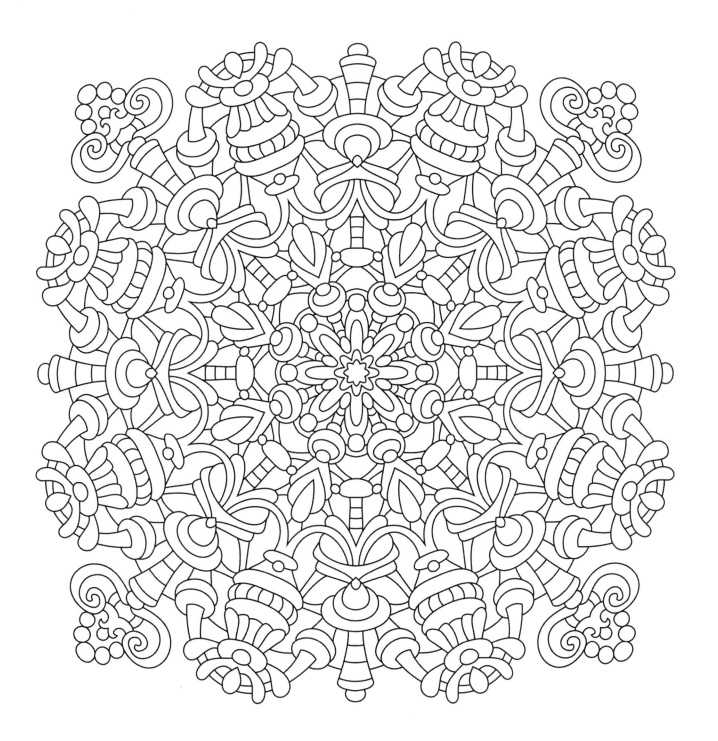

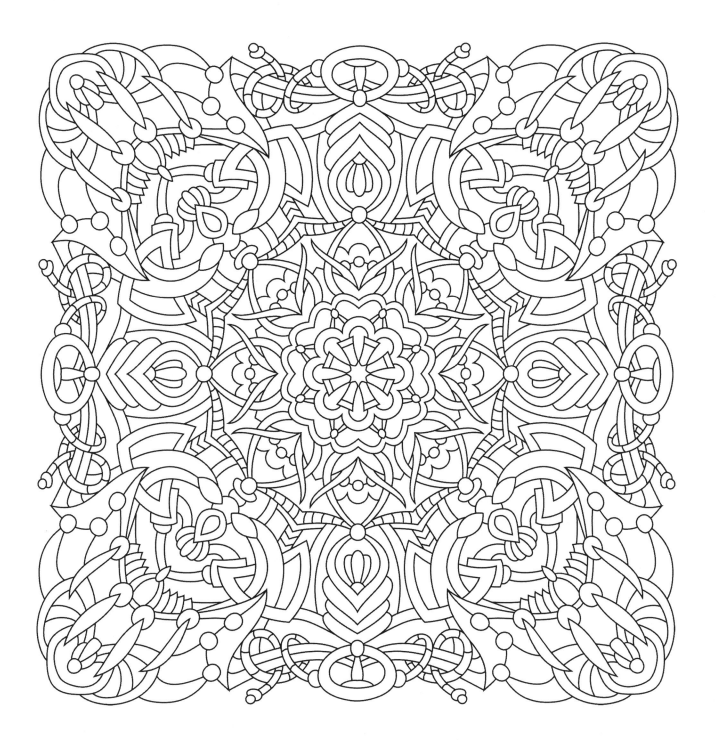

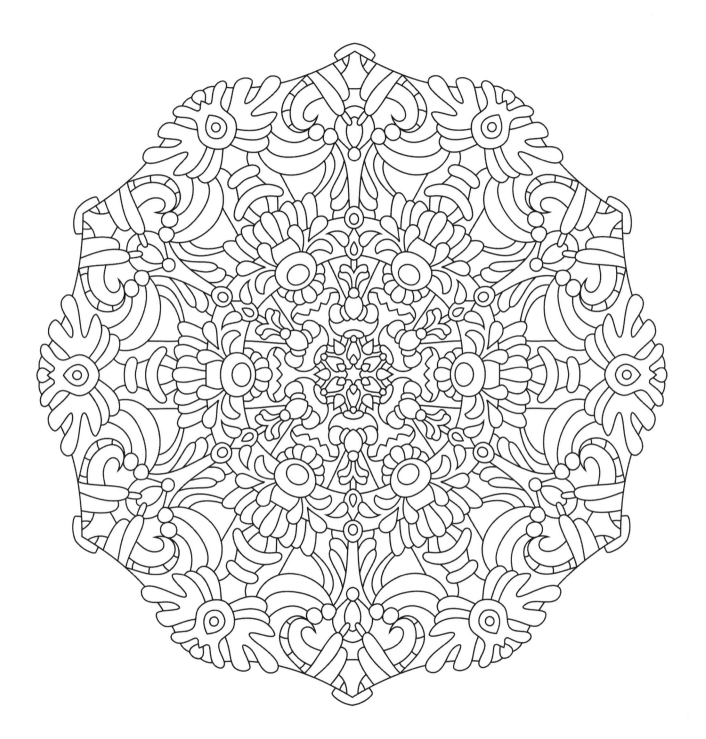

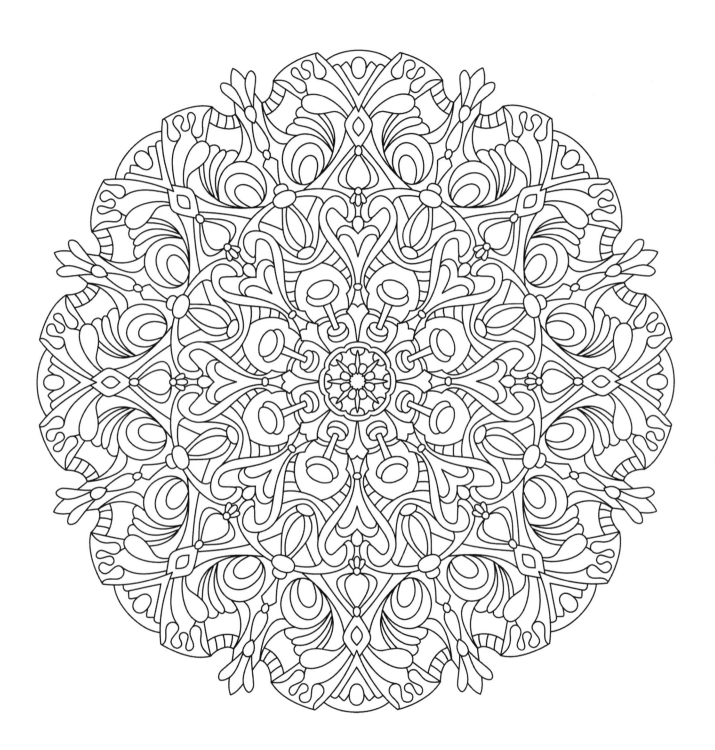

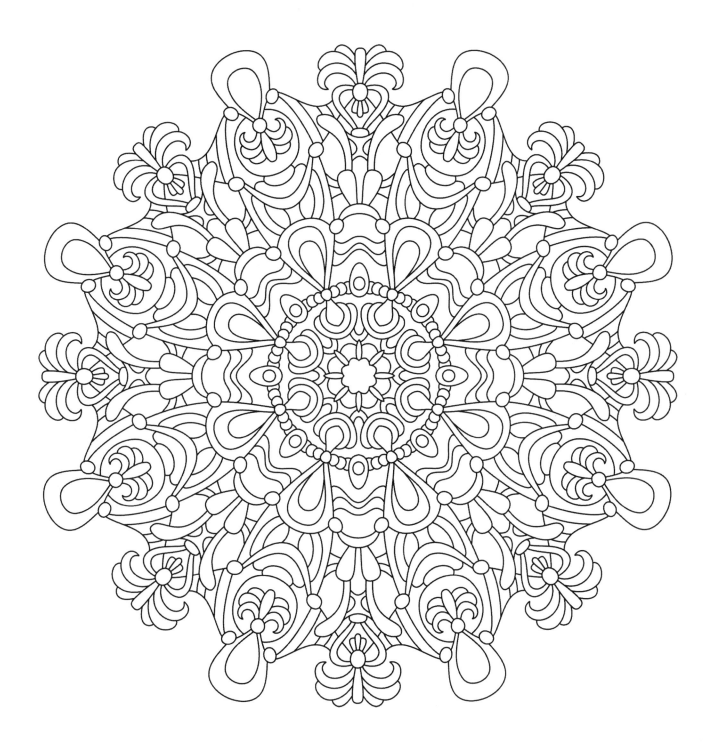

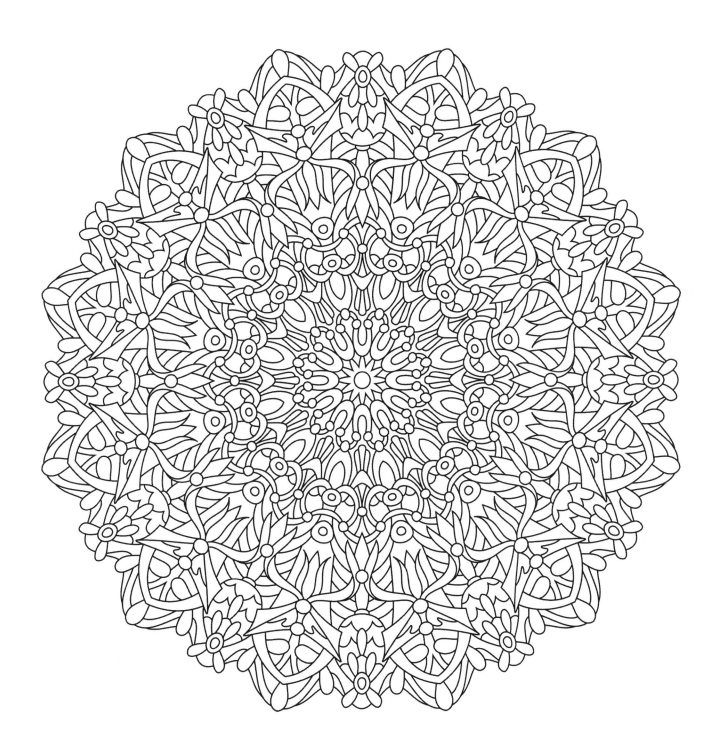

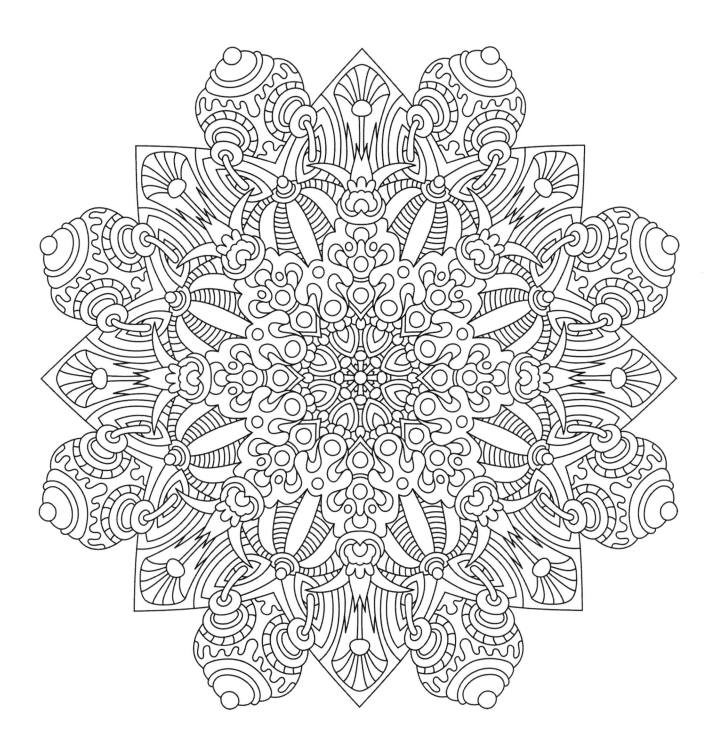

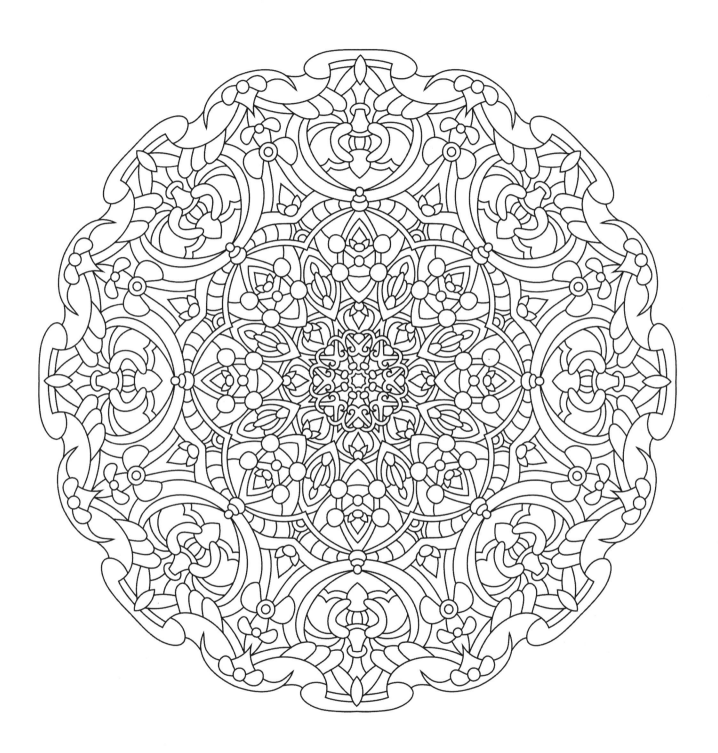

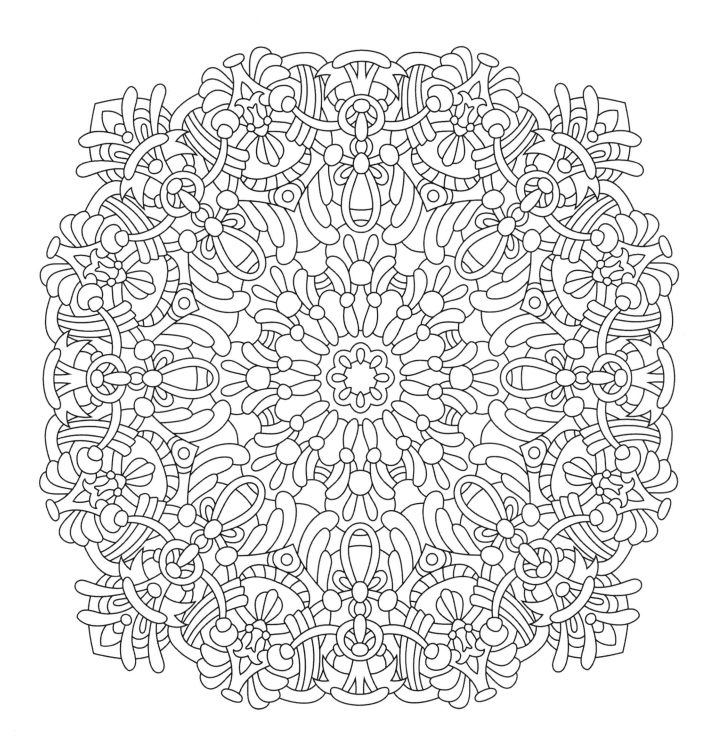

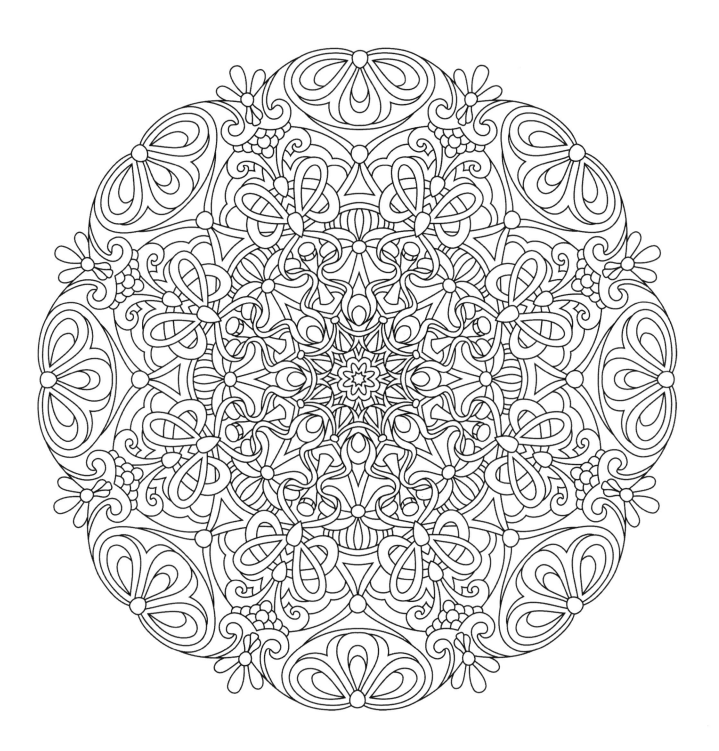

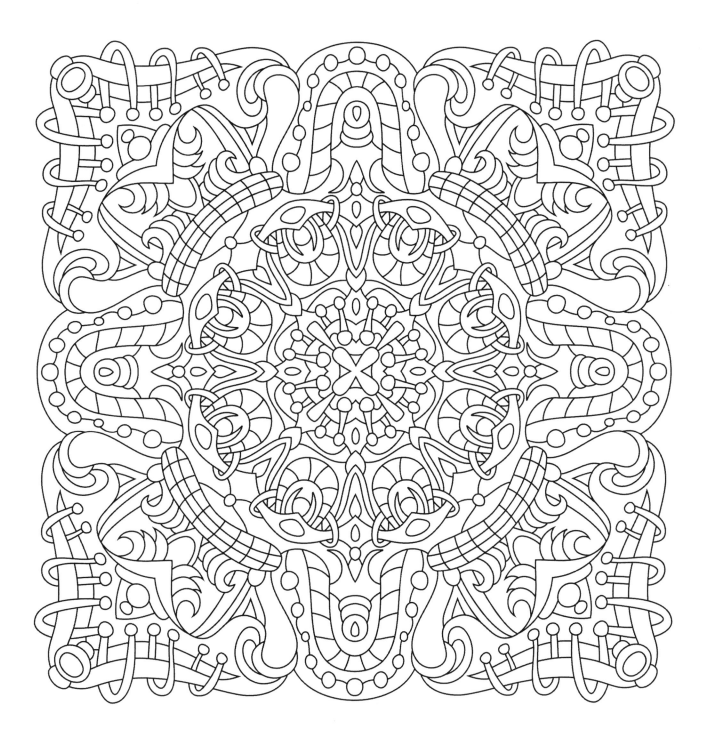

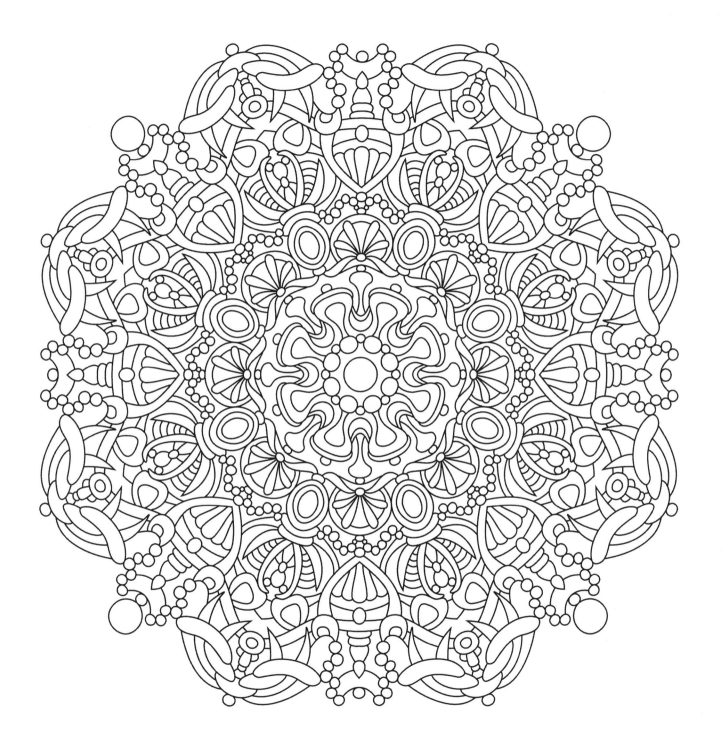

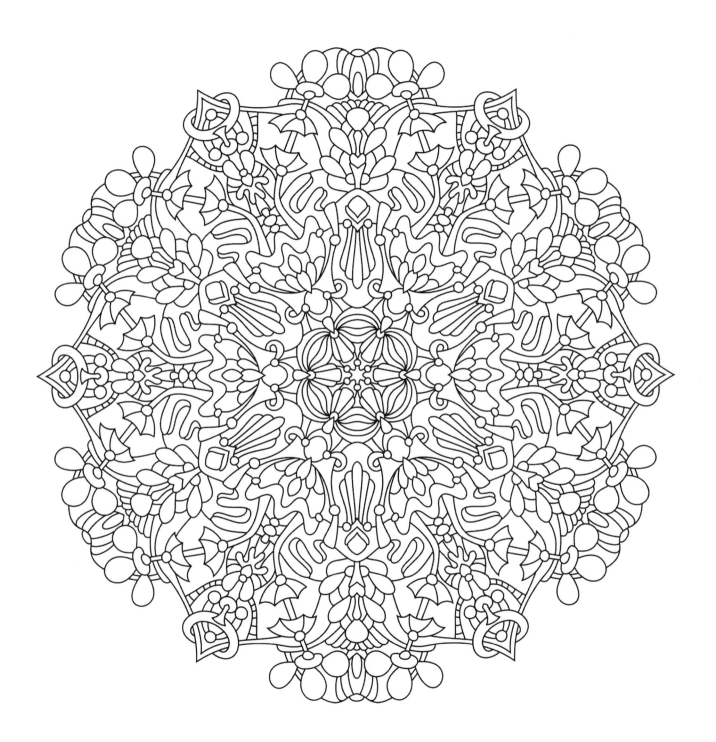

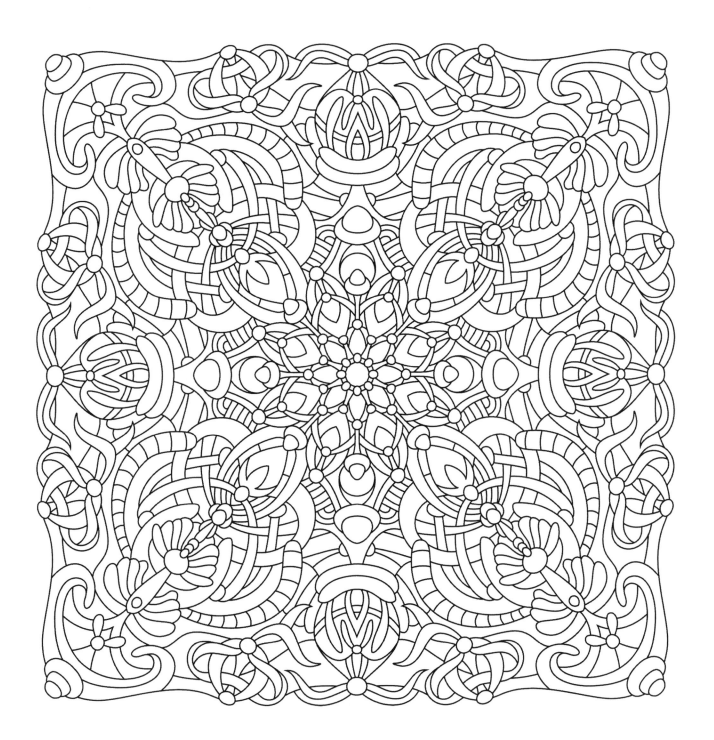

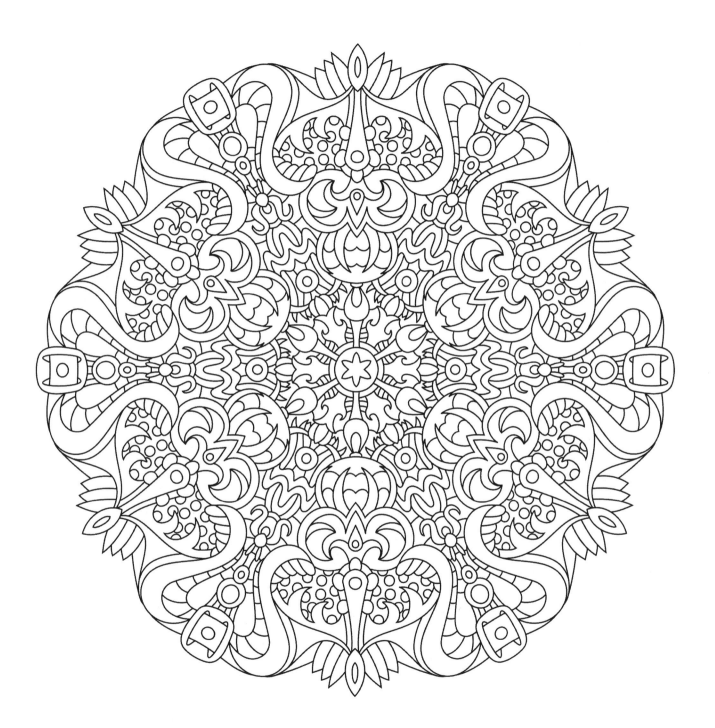

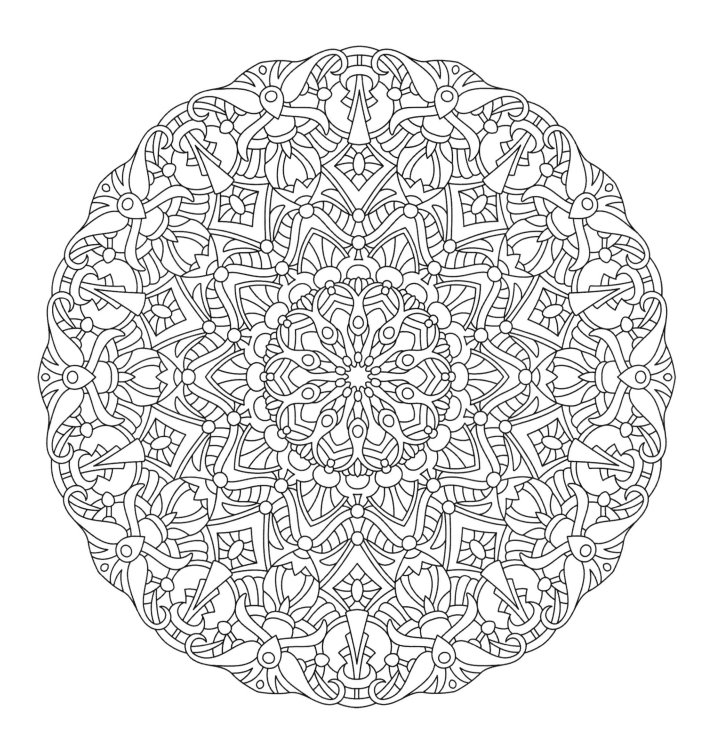

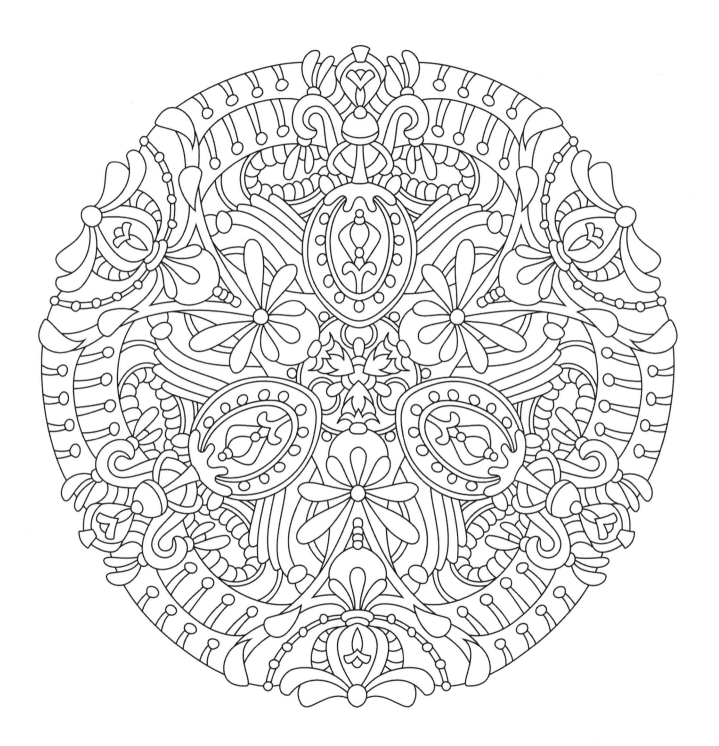

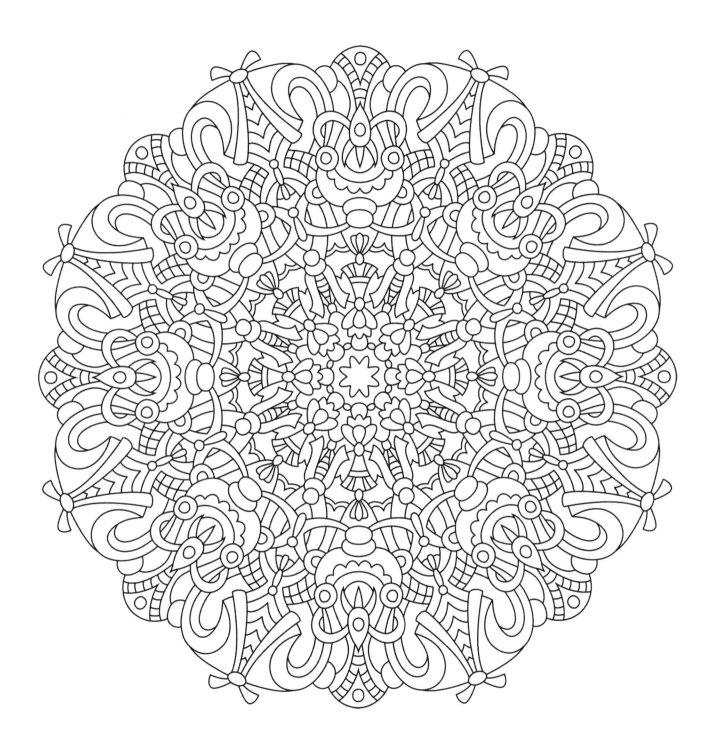

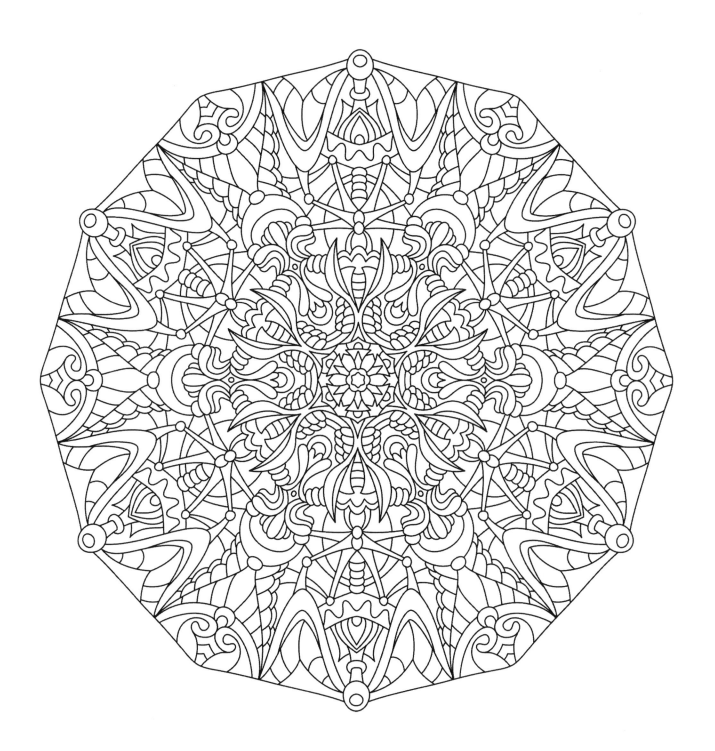

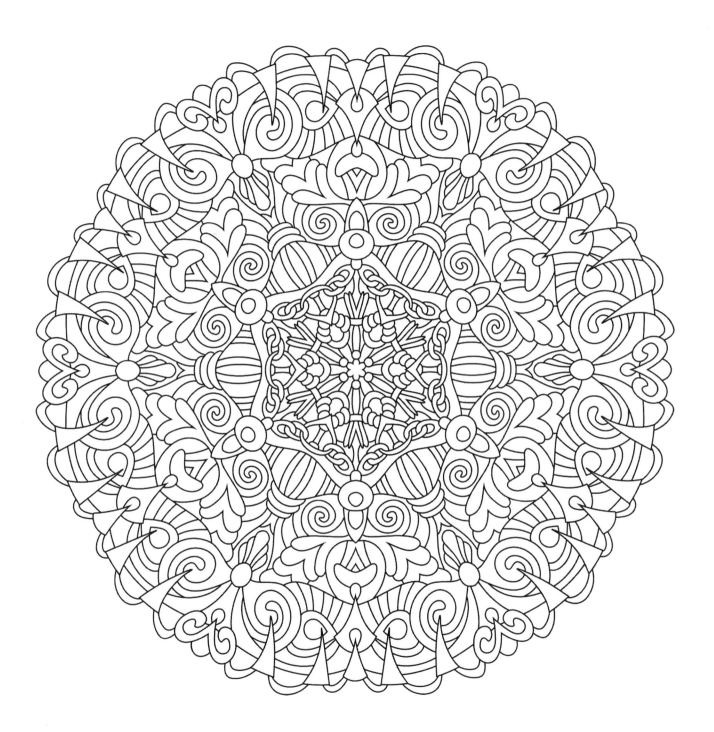

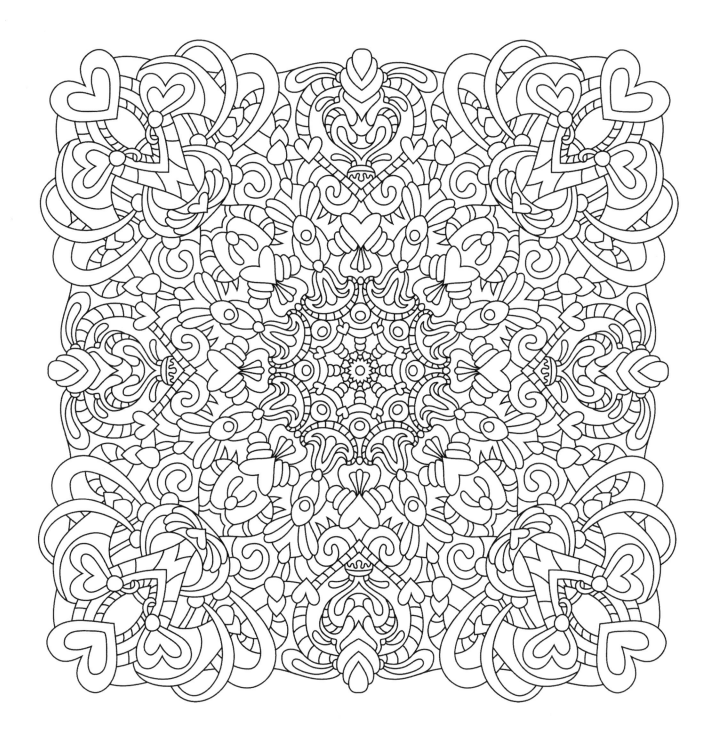

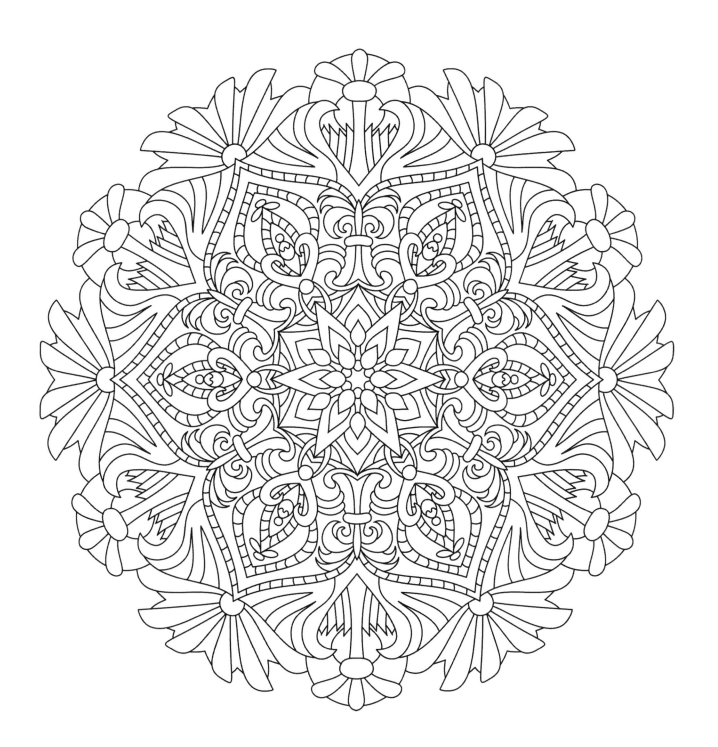

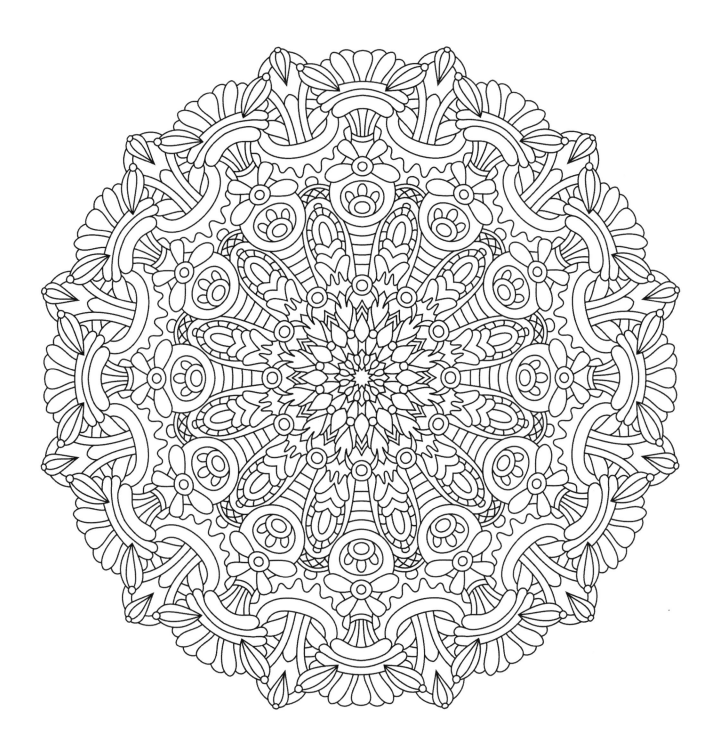

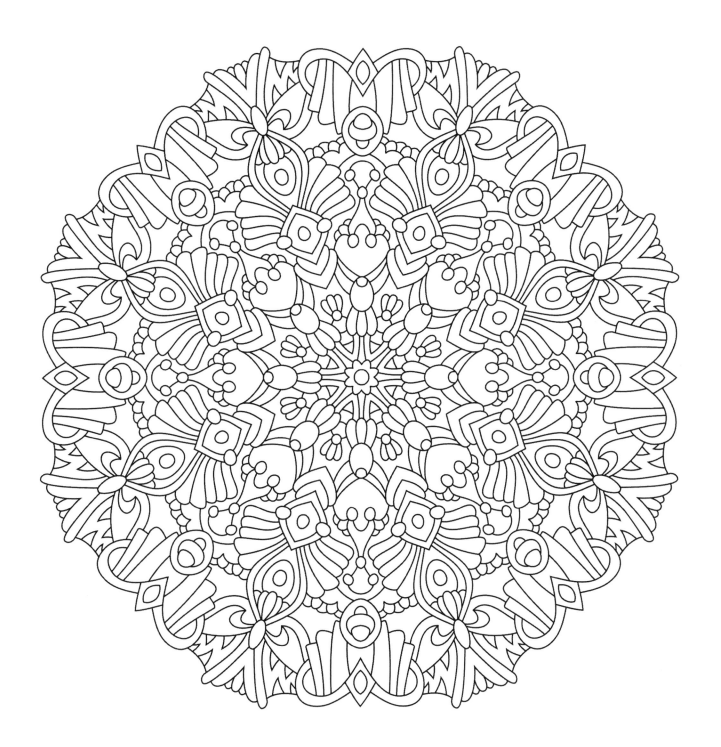

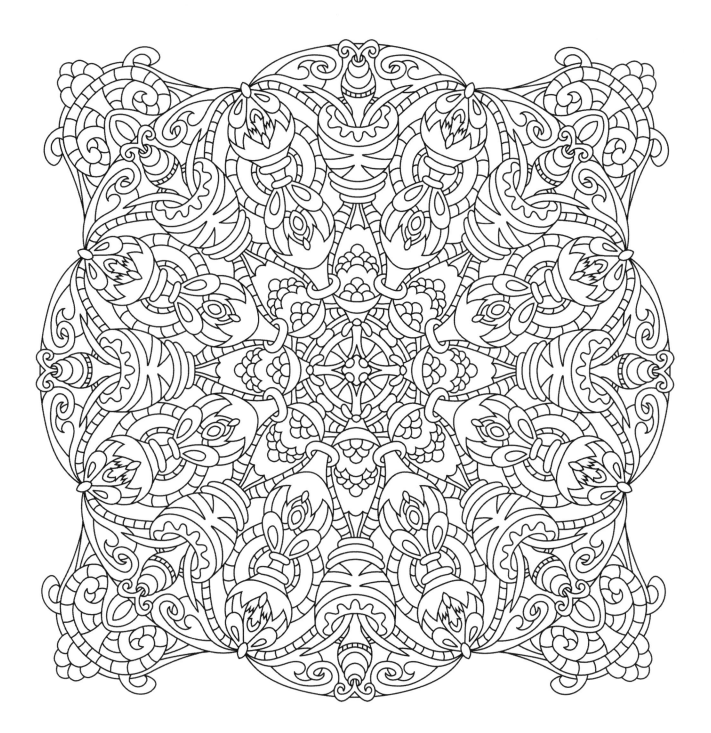

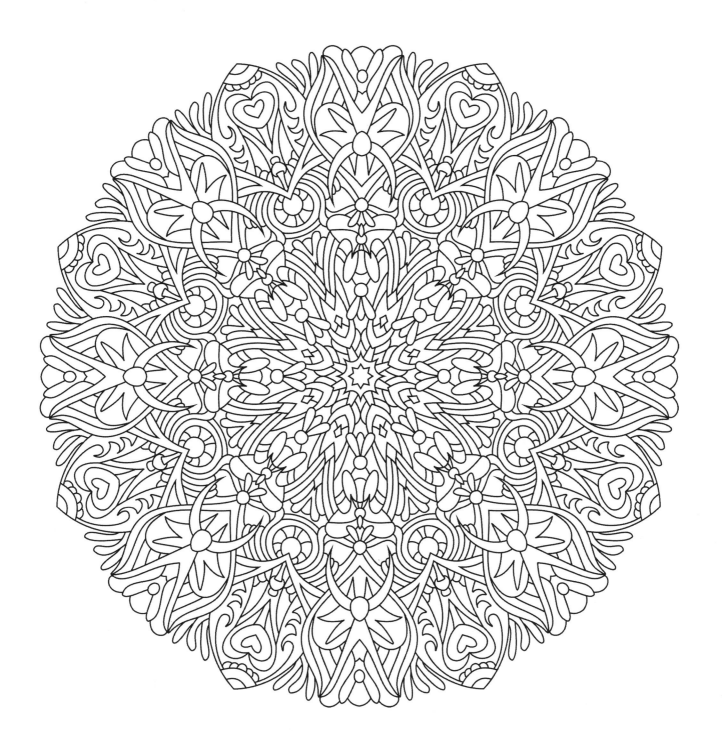

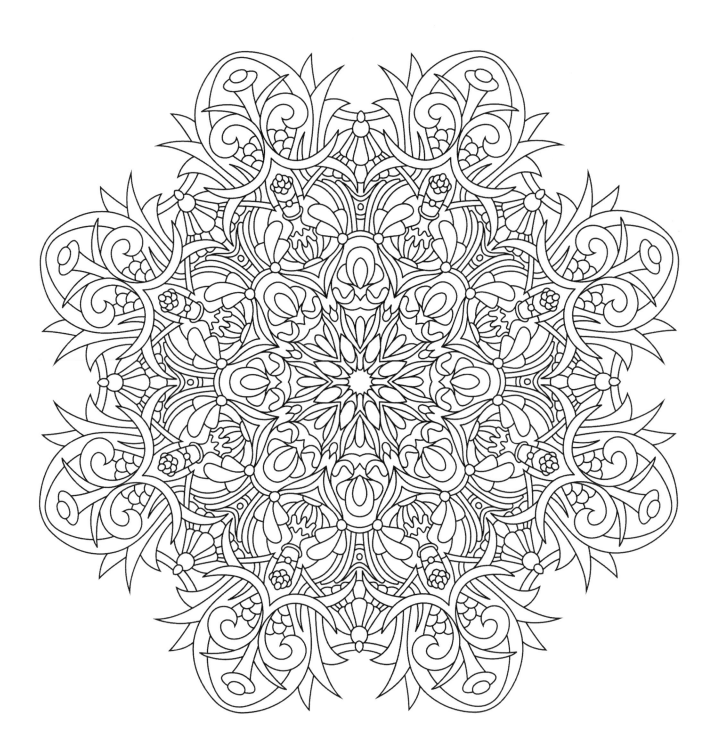

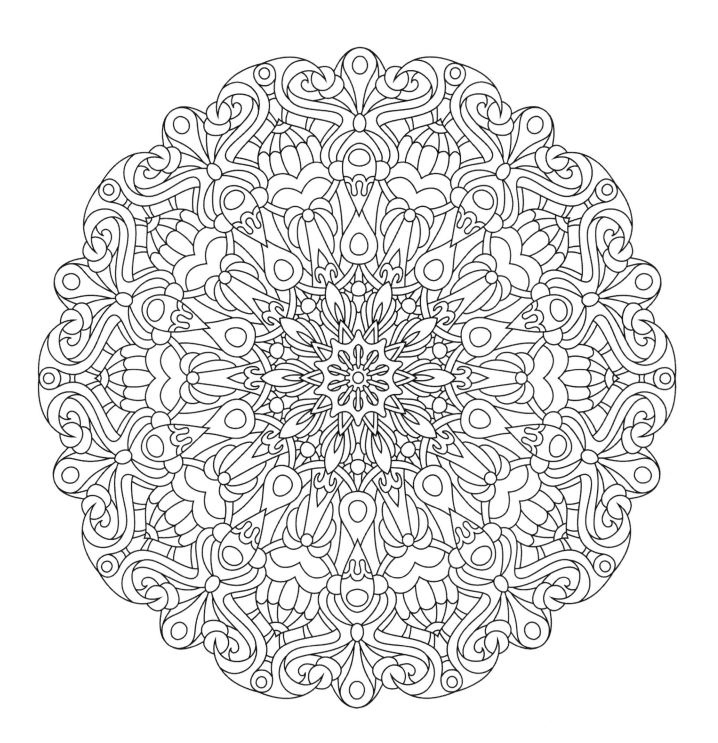

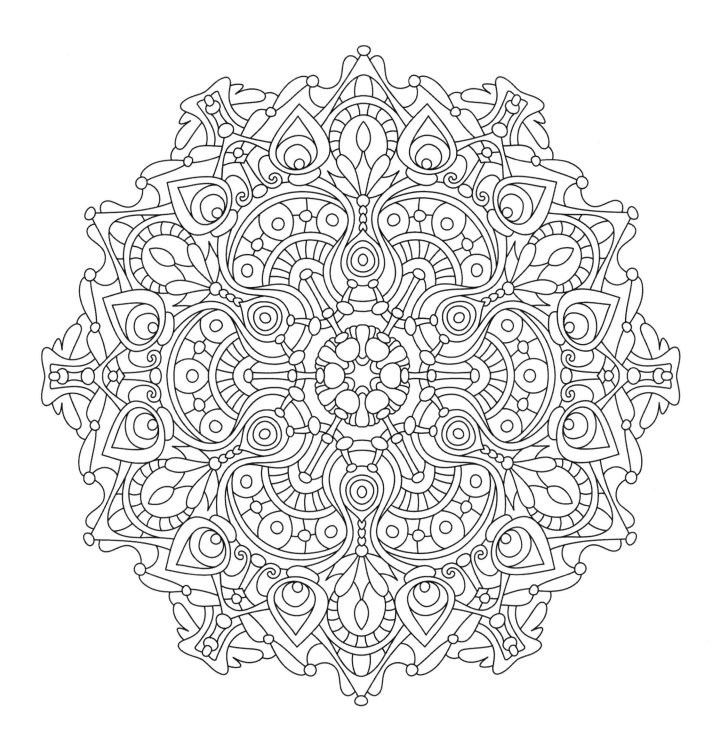

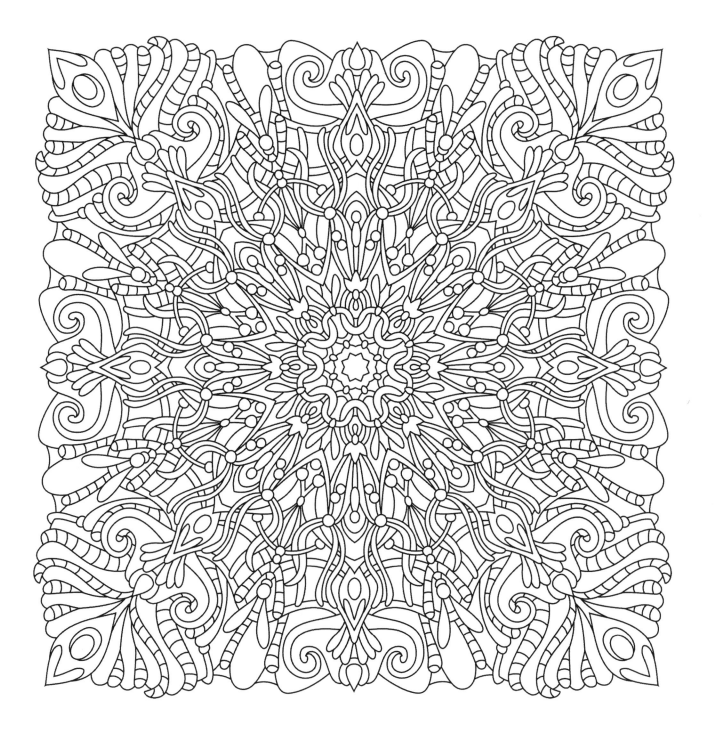

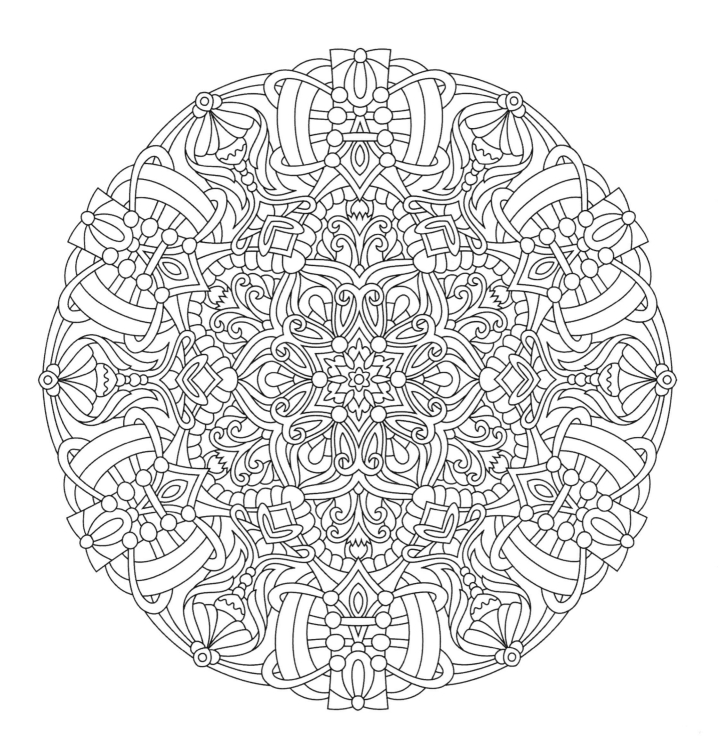

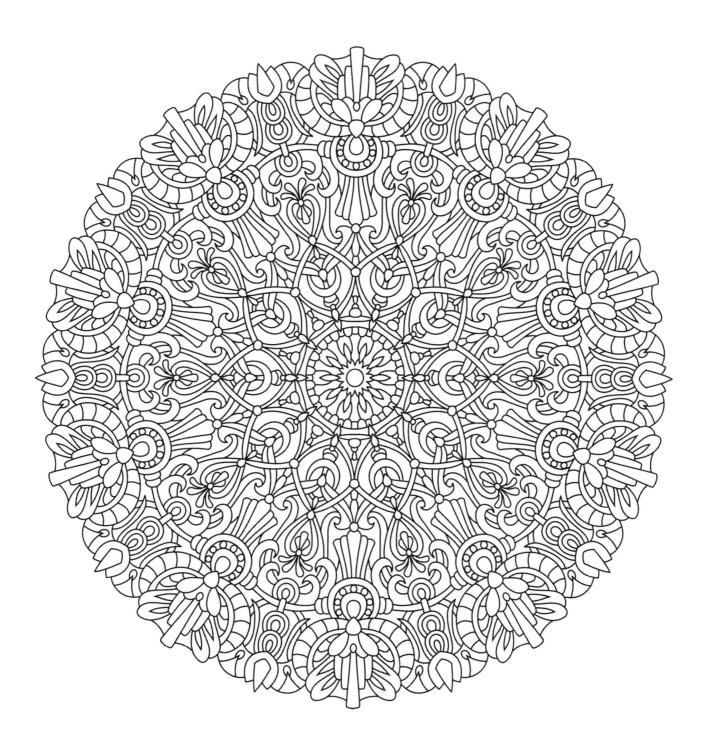

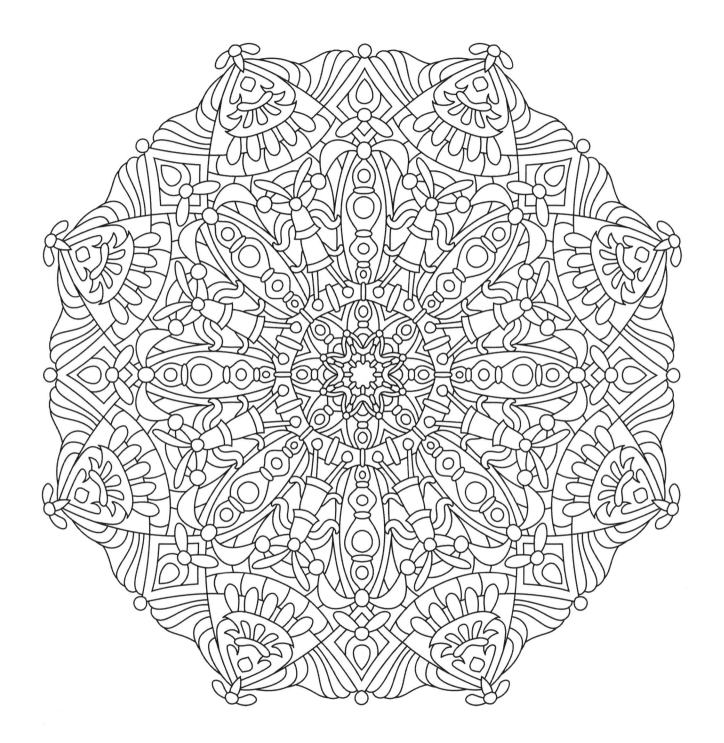

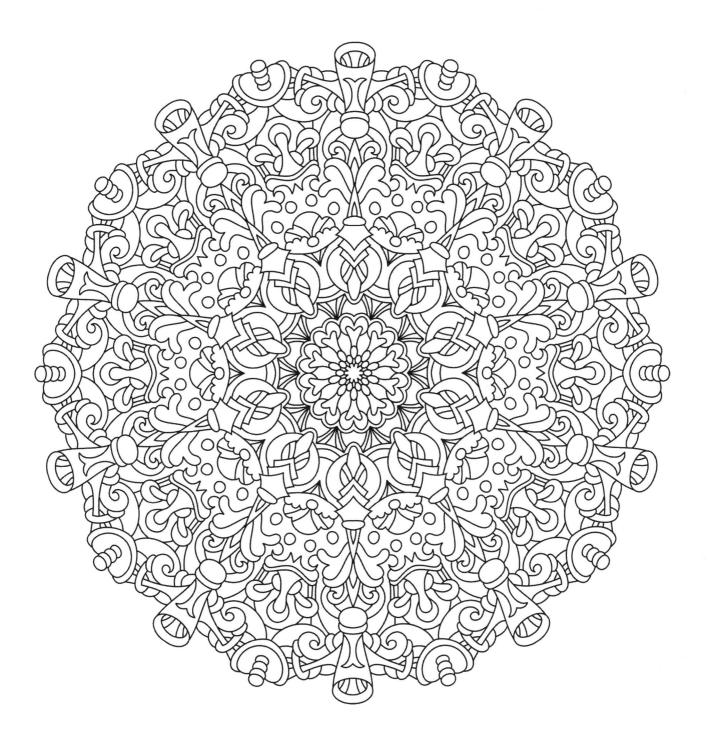

Visit Angie's website
for special web exclusives for colorists.

www.AngieGrace.com

13720231R00059

Printed in Great Britain
by Amazon.co.uk, Ltd.,
Marston Gate.